MY BACKYARD
Garden

MY BACKYARD
Garden

CAROL LERNER

Morrow Junior Books

New York

For May, who knows the secrets of plant life

Watercolors and pencils were used for the full-color illustrations.
The text type is 14-point Sabon.

Published by Morrow Junior Books
a division of William Morrow and Company, Inc.
1350 Avenue of the Americas, New York, NY 10019
http://www.williammorrow.com

Printed in Singapore at Tien Wah Press.

1   2   3   4   5   6   7   8   9   10

Library of Congress Cataloging-in-Publication Data
Lerner, Carol.
My backyard garden/Carol Lerner.
p. cm.
Includes index.
Summary: Explains how to start your own vegetable garden and how to cope with common problems,
describing the round of activities from month to month throughout the year.
ISBN 0-688-14755-0 (trade)—ISBN 0-688-14756-9 (library)
1. Vegetable gardening—Juvenile literature.   2. Vegetables—Juvenile literature.   [1. Vegetable gardening.   2. Gardening.]   I. Title.
SB324.L47 1998   635—dc21   97-6460   CIP AC

CONTENTS

A GARDEN OF YOUR OWN

If you have a little spot of sunny ground, you can enjoy growing some of your own vegetables.

Making a vegetable garden soon brings rewards. You'll harvest snappy vegetables and crisp salads straight from the backyard, raised by your own hands. And they'll taste so much better than supermarket produce!

There's more to making a garden than just putting seeds into the ground. Preparing the soil for planting is hard work, and keeping the garden healthy requires some attention and care week after week. But as you work among your plants, you'll have the pleasure of watching them grow and flourish, all summer long.

My Backyard Garden tells how to start your own garden and how to cope with some common problems you may run into during your gardening year. For special challenges you may need help from local experts. If you have family members or neighbors who garden, be sure to ask them for advice. The "Resources" section on page 46 tells you where to find more help.

The book follows the round of gardening activities from month to month. The order of chores—from planting to harvest—will be the same wherever you live. However, keep in mind that the time when you can begin to work the soil in spring and the dates when it is safe to plant certain seeds or plants depend upon your location. In this book, the last spring frost is assumed to come during the month of May. In the warmer climates of the southern United States, gardeners will be ahead of this schedule by one month or even two. You will need to know the safe planting dates in your own area for each kind of vegetable you grow. The map on page 25 shows the *average* times of the last spring frost in the United States and southern Canada. Local sources described in the "Resources" section can provide more exact information about temperatures in the area where you live.

Happy gardening!

GETTING STARTED

CHOOSING A SITE FOR YOUR GARDEN

Sunlight

Most vegetable plants need a lot of sunshine to grow well. When choosing a location for your garden, look for a spot that has at least six hours of direct summer sun. Eight hours is even better. Stay away from buildings or trees if you can—both make shadows, and tree roots soak up soil moisture and leave your garden dry.

If your backyard has less sunlight, you may still be able to grow some vegetables. Plants grown for their fruits (see "Vegetable Fruits" below), such as tomatoes and peppers, need the most light. Carrots, radishes, and other vegetables grown for their roots can manage on a half day of sunlight, and leafy vegetables (lettuce, spinach) can grow with even less.

VEGETABLE FRUITS

Botany, the study of plants, has its own language.

Somewhere in the center of a flower is a *pistil*, the female organ of the flower. Part of the pistil is an *ovary*, which holds the *ovules* of the plant.

Stamens, the male organs of a flower, produce powdery *pollen*. After the flower is fertilized by pollen, the ovules become *seeds*, and the ovary ripens into a *fruit*. A tomato or a pepper or a green bean is a fruit (a ripened ovary) containing seeds (the ripened ovules).

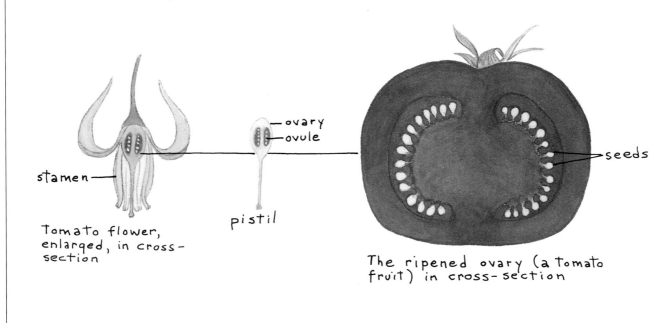

stamen

Tomato flower, enlarged, in cross-section

ovary
ovule

pistil

seeds

The ripened ovary (a tomato fruit) in cross-section

Water

Plants need water to grow, but too much can kill them. Look for a spot with good drainage.

Excess water drains away from plants on a gentle slope. But on steep slopes, the rain runs off so quickly that it washes away the garden soil.

If the ground is flat and puddles remain there after a rainstorm, you might be able to improve the drainage by making a raised bed. You can use soil raked up from the garden paths or a bag or two of topsoil bought from a garden center. Pile up the earth in the bed (the space where the plants will grow) so it is at least a few inches higher than the area around it.

Making a raised bed

Make sure that you have a source of water nearby. When plants are young, and whenever the soil becomes dry, you will have to water your garden.

HOW BIG?

If this is your first garden, think small. Big gardens require a lot of work, and even a small space can hold a large number of plants. Twenty square feet (four feet by five feet) is a good size for a starter garden. Even if you're willing to spend a lot of time gardening, you probably should not start with a plot larger than eight feet by ten feet.

MAKING A PLAN

After you choose your site, make a plan for your garden. Draw a map of your garden space to scale, allowing one inch or a half inch for each foot of space. Then decide where your crops will go. Here are some things to think about as you plan:

- What do you want to grow? There's no point in planting vegetables you don't like to eat (although you may find that some taste better when they're home-grown!).
- Some fast-growing vegetables can be planted in early spring. Others need warmer weather and soil and won't survive outdoors until later in the season. You should be able to use some of your space twice by planting a second crop after harvesting an early one. This won't work if you live where the growing season is *very* short, or when a cold, wet spring delays your early planting.

- Put tall plants, such as tomatoes and pole beans, on the north side of the garden, where they won't shade the others.
- Some plants, such as squashes, are space hogs, but you can still grow them in a small garden if you give them support so they grow upward instead of on the ground. Or, if your parents don't mind, you can try growing them in a corner of your garden and letting them ramble over the lawn.

EASY VEGETABLES FOR	
EARLY PLANTING	LATE PLANTING
beets	basil
cabbages	beans
carrots	cucumbers
leaf lettuce	eggplants
onions	peppers
parsley	pumpkins
peas	summer squashes
radishes	(zucchini, patty-
spinach	pan, crookneck,
turnips	and so on)
	tomatoes

Seed catalogs are basic reference books for gardeners. They list the varieties of vegetables that are available and the characteristics of each. Here are some questions the catalog can answer:

- Does this plant have built-in resistance to common plant diseases?
- Does the plant need a lot of space? Some kinds of beans, peas, cucumbers, and squashes are bushy, while others grow as vines. Unless you can let the vines sprawl, you will have to give them support.
- How long will it take before the vegetable is ready to pick? For instance, one variety of tomato ripens after fifty days in the garden, while another needs eighty. If you live where the growing season is short, this information will help you choose the varieties that are right for your area.

Seeds from catalogs can be expensive because of shipping and handling charges, but many companies will send a catalog without charge if you ask for one. Look in the winter issues of garden magazines at your public library to find catalog offers.

Two sample garden plans are shown on the next four pages. Of course, a garden doesn't have to be a square or a rectangle. Use a round bed or any area of sunny space you have. In these sample plans, most of the garden space is used twice—to grow an early spring crop and then a later summer one.

These gardens are planted in wide beds rather than single rows. Single rows of vegetables separated by pathways waste a lot of garden space. With wide beds, you use more space for planting and less for paths. That way you can plant double or even triple rows of some plants in the same bed. If the seed package instructions say that full-grown lettuce plants, for example, should stand eight inches apart, you can plant a second row of lettuce just eight inches away from the first row in the same bed.

PAUL'S GARDEN (4 FEET BY 5 FEET)

SPRING GARDEN

Most of the plants in this garden plan will be ready for harvest within two months of planting. The sugar peas will need one additional month. Everything is planted from seeds.

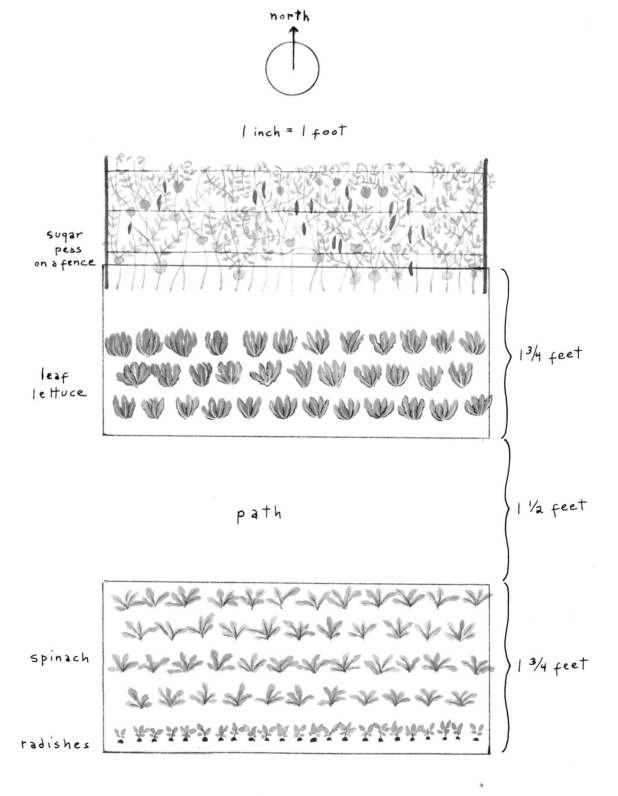

north

1 inch = 1 foot

sugar peas on a fence

leaf lettuce

1 ¾ feet

path

1 ½ feet

spinach

radishes

1 ¾ feet

SUMMER GARDEN

These plants go into the ground after there is no further danger of frost. Peppers, tomatoes, basil, and marigolds go into the garden as young plants; the others are planted from seeds. The peas stay in place until they finish producing. When they stop, the plants are removed, and lettuce is planted in their place.

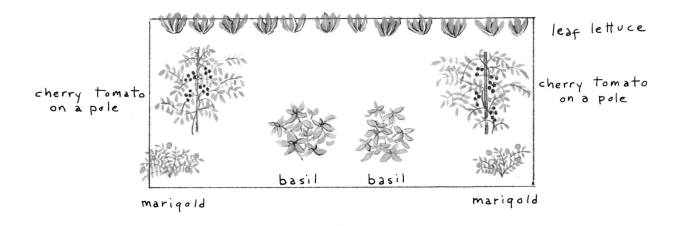

leaf lettuce

cherry tomato on a pole

cherry tomato on a pole

basil   basil

mariqold   mariqold

bush beans

pepper   pepper

mariqold   mariqold

LORI'S GARDEN (8 FEET BY 10 FEET)

SPRING GARDEN
The cabbages and parsley are bought as young plants; the onions are planted as sets (small bulbs that are sold in garden shops in early spring). All the other vegetables are planted from seeds.

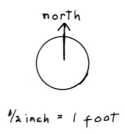

north

½ inch = 1 foot

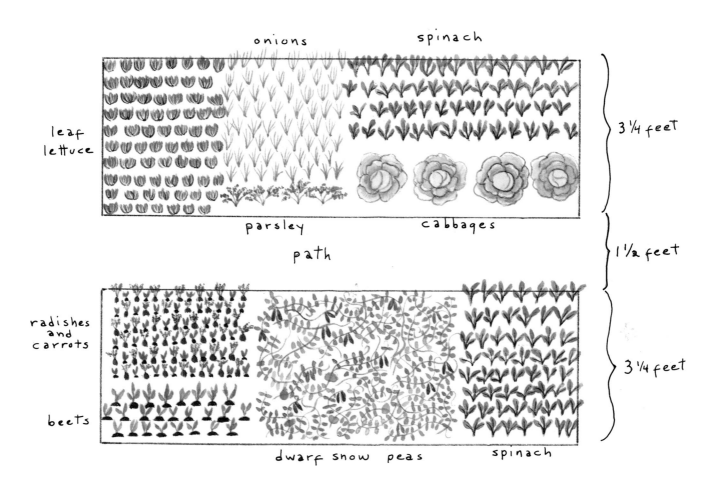

SUMMER GARDEN

Basil, eggplants, tomatoes, and zinnias are put in as young plants; everything else is planted from seeds. The parsley keeps growing all summer. When Lori's frost-free date comes, all the spring lettuce and spinach are harvested and the summer vegetables planted in their place. The cabbages, carrots, beets, snow peas, and the last of the onions are harvested a month later and their space replanted then.

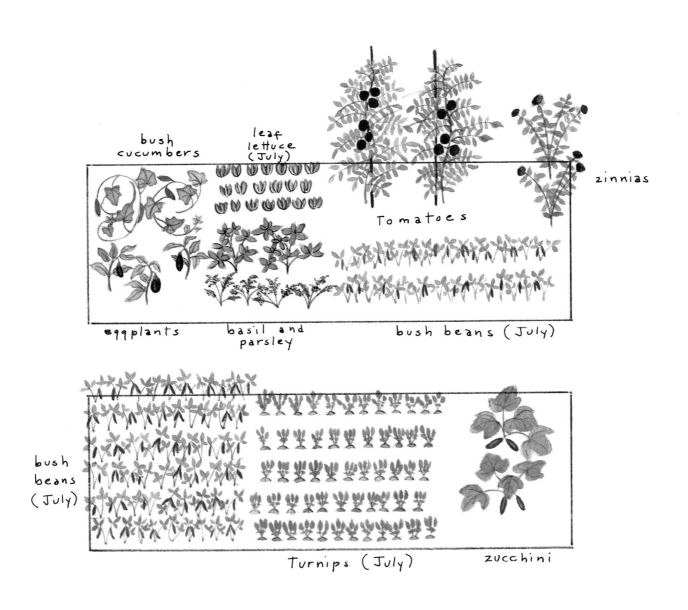

bush cucumbers

leaf lettuce (July)

zinnias

Tomatoes

eggplants

basil and parsley

bush beans (July)

bush beans (July)

Turnips (July)

zucchini

KEEPING A RECORD

The best gardening lessons come from your own experiences. Start a notebook now to record the history of your garden. Copy the garden plan into the notebook as the first entry. Make a note of the plant varieties you buy, and mark down the dates when you put in seeds or plants and when you start harvesting each vegetable. If you have problems or unusual weather conditions, write that down too.

TOOLS

You will need a few tools to start your garden. A spading fork or a shovel is needed for turning the soil, and a steel rake is helpful for smoothing the beds.

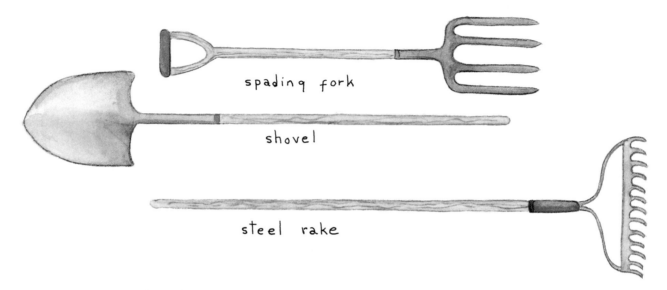

Hoes are used to break up clods of earth and to scrape young weeds from the ground, but a hand cultivator is better for weed control in a small garden. When putting in young plants, you can make holes with a trowel, your hands, a large mixing spoon, or a stick. A watering can that pours the water out in a spray is best, because it won't wash away the soil around newly planted seeds or tiny seedlings.

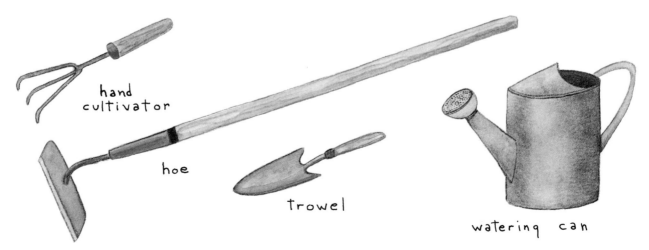

Finally, you will need some old clothes that won't be ruined by dirt.

Before you start working, develop a few habits of tool safety. Spading forks, shovels, rakes, hoes, and cultivators do their jobs best when their edges are sharp. Protect yourself and others by handling them safely. When you lay a tool on the ground, always turn the sharp edge downward. Wear shoes when using tools to avoid cuts and bruises on your feet. When you dig or hoe or do other heavy work, put on a pair of work gloves to protect your hands from blisters. And if you attack weeds with a hand tool, always keep the other hand away from the target area.

PREPARING THE GROUND

This is the hardest part of making a garden, but one of the most important.

Begin by measuring out your garden space with a yardstick or tape measure. To mark the borders, push sticks into the ground at the corners and run string between them.

If you are working on a spot that has been gardened before, you're lucky. In that case, the ground has already been broken, and you need only loosen the soil and remove weeds that have crept in. But if yours is a new garden area, you may have to break up hard soil and clear out a jungle of grass and weedy plants.

Lawns are the hardest areas to prepare because grass roots twist together to make a thick mat. You need to remove as much of the root layer as you can, so you won't have grass springing up among your vegetables. Use a shovel to skim off the grass along with the top inch or so of soil, which contains the roots. As you dig out the grass clumps, set them aside to put in the compost pile (see page 20). You may need help from an adult to do this job.

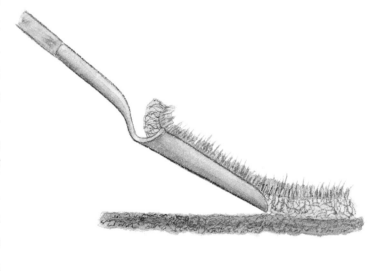

Removing grass

Try to dig up the soil as deeply as you can—eight inches is good. Then break up the big clods with a hand cultivator or a hoe and take out stones and any more weeds or grass roots. These weeds and roots will go into the compost pile too.

Plants thrive when their roots receive a good balance of moisture and minerals. After removing the weeds and lumps, you can take some steps to improve the soil. First you will need to figure out what kind of soil you have.

Soil Texture

Take a handful of earth and rub it through your fingers. Soil that contains a lot of clay feels slippery and greasy and sticks to your fingers. Soil that has a lot of sand in it is gritty and doesn't hold together in a ball when it's wet the way clay soil does.

Clay is made up of very small particles. It holds lots of water, but there isn't much room for air between the particles. Plant roots need both moisture and air to grow well.

Sand particles are large, so there is plenty of air space between them. But water drains through the spaces quickly, leaving the soil dry.

Ideal garden soil is silt. Its particles are in between clay and sand in size, and it holds both air and water well.

TESTING SOIL TEXTURE

Fill a cup with dry soil from different parts of your garden. Break up the lumps, remove any roots or stones, and put the soil in a jar. Add a teaspoon of dishwasher detergent, fill the jar with water, and screw on the lid. Shake the jar until everything is mixed together and then set the jar down.

The heavy sand particles will settle out in the first minutes. Let the jar sit for a few days until all the soil particles have settled out of the water. You will see a layer of silt above the coarse sand at the bottom and a layer of fine clay on top of the silt.

If half or more of the soil in the jar is clay or sand, that is your soil type. If the three kinds of particles are equal or if silt makes up a large proportion, you have loam soil—which is the best.

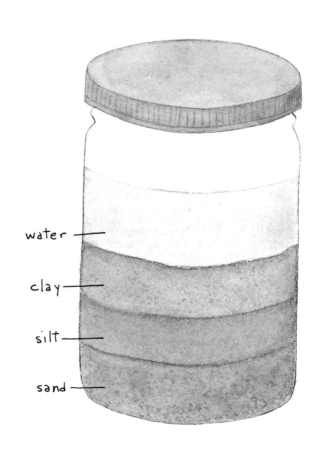

Chemical Tests

Soil acidity determines how well your plants will be able to take up nutrients from the soil. Acidity is measured by a pH test, which rates soil on a scale of 1 to 14. Low numbers mean the soil is acidic; soil with ratings above 7 is called alkaline.

Most vegetables do best in soil rated between 6 and 7.5. By adding lime to acid soils or sulfur to alkaline ones, gardeners can move their soil into the desired pH range.

You can measure pH yourself by using litmus paper. Your school science teacher may be able to give you a few strips of litmus paper so you can do the test. Or you can buy a home testing kit from a garden store.

Testing by a laboratory will provide more exact ratings. Many county and state Extension Service offices do soil testing for a small fee (see "Resources," page 46). Private laboratories usually charge more.

A laboratory test will also analyze the amount of plant nutrients (nitrogen, phosphorus, and potassium) available in your soil. Knowing that, you will know what is needed to improve it.

Understanding your soil will make you a more scientific gardener, but many people garden successfully for years without ever having done a soil test. If you add lots of good organic matter and some fertilizer to your garden (see pages 20 and 21), it will probably do well even without testing.

There is one exception to this. If you have any reason to think your garden may contain lead, you *must* test before growing vegetables. Lead is a poison that plants absorb from the earth.

Test for lead if your garden site:
- contained painted buildings (Years ago, house paints were made with lead.)
- was or is near a busy road receiving auto exhaust
- was part of an orchard (At one time, orchards were sprayed with insecticides containing lead.)
- was ever used for dumping

Your Extension Service, state Department of Agriculture, or local Public Health Department can tell you where to get tests for lead.

Improving the Soil

Once you know what kind of soil you have, you can start to improve it, if necessary.

Mixing organic matter into your garden improves soil texture: Clay soil will hold more air and drain better, and sandy soil will be able to hold more water. Gardeners use a variety of organic materials—leaves, grass clippings, kitchen scraps, manure from livestock, and so on. Many organic materials are also natural fertilizers, containing chemicals that plants need for healthy growth.

But the organic materials won't help your garden until they begin to decay. After they have rotted, they turn into a dark crumbly material called compost or humus. It doesn't have a bad smell, and it's gold dust for your garden.

Most gardeners set up a compost pile where they can toss all their plant wastes and let them rot. The pile can be out of sight somewhere in a corner of the yard. A simple enclosure will keep it neat. A ring of fence wire or snow fencing makes a good container and allows air into the pile. It may take a few weeks or as long as a year for the pile to decay. Chopping up the plants before adding them to the pile will speed the action. So will "turning" the pile—stirring and mixing the materials with a shovel or spading fork. High temperatures and moisture, and an occasional addition of manure or other fertilizer, make it decompose faster too. But sooner or later, the material will decay, and you will have compost.

compost heap with fence wire

compost heap with snow fence

Some kinds of waste should *not* go into the compost heap—meat and bones, dog and cat manure, diseased plants, weed seeds, and clippings from a lawn that was treated with herbicides.

Some communities sell or give away compost in connection with their recycling programs. You can buy peat moss, dried manure, and some other organic materials in garden stores.

Unless you have plenty of compost, you will need fertilizer to nourish your plants. Natural fertilizers such as manures improve soil by adding organic matter, but they may not contain a balance of all the nutrients that plants need. Some garden stores sell blended organic fertilizers—a mix of natural ingredients containing a broad range of nutrients.

Unlike organic fertilizers, chemical fertilizers do nothing to improve soil texture. However, they work fast and they provide a more complete supply of nutrients than any single natural fertilizer. Unlike organic fertilizers, they may actually do harm if they come into *direct* contact with the plants. If you use them, always work the fertilizer thoroughly into the soil before planting.

You will see three numbers printed on a package of fertilizer. They tell the percentage of each of three important nutrients found in the product. The first number refers to nitrogen (N), the second to phosphate (P), and the third to potash (K).

In buying a blended organic fertilizer, look for one that contains roughly equal amounts of the three. The numbers for each nutrient will be much lower than they are on a bag of chemical fertilizer. Chemical fertilizers coded 10-10-10 or 5-10-5 are good for general-purpose use in the vegetable garden.

Handle chemical fertilizer carefully, as you would any chemical. Wait for a day without wind, so the fertilizer doesn't blow away. Use a scoop to spread it on the garden. Keep it away from your face and eyes, and wash your hands when you finish. Then use a rake or hoe to mix the fertilizer into the top few inches of soil.

INVADERS: DOGS, CATS, AND WILDLIFE

Every garden attracts some unwelcome insects. In the pages ahead, you will find suggestions for protecting your plants from some of the most common insect pests. Four-footed animals can ruin a garden too, and birds sometimes peck out the seeds of young plants.

If you discover that your plants are under attack, the first step is to identify the culprit. You may have to make a stakeout in your yard at nightfall, or just before dawn, when many animals are out feeding. Once you know the invader, you can take steps to stop the destruction.

Rabbits nibble on lettuce and other greens and on young shoots. You may be able to discourage them by shaking ground pepper around young plants. A sure solution is a two-foot-high fence of chicken wire. The bottom of the fence must be snug against the ground so the rabbit can't crawl underneath.

Raccoons aren't usually a problem unless you grow corn, but it is very hard to keep them out of a corn patch. Some people have succeeded by planting squashes around the corn and between the rows. Raccoons seem to dislike walking among the prickly squash leaves. Other gardeners catch them in live traps and take the captives to a distant forest to set them free. A fence won't stop them unless it is a wire one at least four feet tall, with the top eighteen inches of fence wire unattached to the fence poles. When the raccoon climbs to the top, its weight causes the fence wire to bend backward, and the animal drops off.

Squirrels sometimes develop a taste for tomatoes, taking a bite or two from each one. They are less likely to reach tomatoes growing on a wide-mesh wire fence. Choose a tall (rather than bushy) variety and tie it to the fence as it grows. Tall varieties are described as "indeterminate" on seed packages and in catalogs. Indeterminate tomatoes behave like vines: The tips of these plants keep growing longer and longer until the weather becomes unfavorable.

If you suspect that deer might raid the yard, try to discourage them before they get the first taste. The smell of perfumed bar soap or of human hair, stuffed into plastic mesh bags or old nylon stockings and hung around the garden, may repel them. Some people sprinkle hot sauce on the ground! But none of these precautions will keep a starving deer from invading. Only a *very* tall fence can do that.

Birds can be destructive too, but they also eat enormous quantities of insects—including many garden pests—during the growing season, so you want them patrolling your yard. In any case, scare devices—a scarecrow, aluminum pans or strips of plastic or foil hung around the garden, and plastic or inflatable snakes or owls—are not very effective. Birds and other animals soon figure out that these props are no threat. If birds pick at seedlings, protect the plants by bending a piece of metal screening or chicken wire into a low tunnel and placing it over the row. When the plants are a few inches tall, you can remove the protection.

The neighbor's dog or cat—or your own pet—may also be a nuisance. Cats sometimes dig in freshly turned earth. A piece of chicken wire laid over the seedbeds until the plants have sprouted will discourage digging. Your own dog may also think that a soft garden patch is an invitation to dig. Try to teach it otherwise. If you can train your pet to respect your garden area, you might discover that your dog is your best defense against other invaders. With their keen sense of smell, the wildlife will be aware of your dog's presence and may choose to avoid an unwelcome meeting.

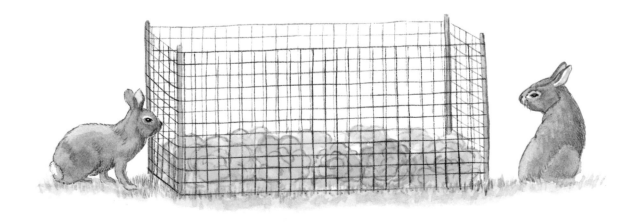

MARCH

Display racks in hardware and garden stores—and even in supermarkets—are filled with packages of fresh garden seeds. If you haven't bought your seeds yet, this is the time to do it.

It's also a good time to set up a compost pile in your yard. Soon you will need a place to put weeds and other garden waste.

March weather is uncertain. Even though the ground is still cold, you can begin planting as soon as the soil is dry enough to work. If you're having a very cold and wet spring, you may have to wait until next month to prepare the soil and start planting. Here is the traditional squeeze test for early spring planting:

Take a handful of soil and squeeze it into a ball. Hold it in your open hand and poke the ball with a finger. If you just make a dent, the soil is too wet. If the ball breaks up and crumbles, it's ready to work.

Once your soil is dry enough, you are ready to prepare the garden beds (see "Preparing the Ground," pages 17 to 21) and plant your first crops. Seed packages have instructions for planting—how to space the seeds in a row and how deep to plant them. A wooden yardstick is handy for planting seeds in rows. Just lay the edge of the yardstick along the row and press it down gently to the desired depth. Then lay the yardstick alongside the furrow you've made and use its markings as a guide for spacing the seeds in the furrow. Cover the seeds (not too deeply!), pat down the soil, and water the ground with a gentle spray.

Some seeds, such as lettuce and carrots, are tiny and hard to handle. If you mix the seeds with a little dry sand, you will find them easier to control. Sow them as evenly as you can and don't worry if they're too crowded. When the seedlings come up, you can thin them for correct spacing by removing the excess plants.

You can pull out the extra plants or else use a small nail scissors to cut them out. If you pull them, do it gently, so you don't disturb the roots of the seedlings you want to keep. Try to save the largest plants and remove the weaker ones. If the seedlings are growing bunched together, press down on the soil at the bottom of the cluster with the fingers of your other hand while pulling out the extras.

The plants listed below not only tolerate cold but grow well *only* in cool weather. They can be planted four to six weeks before the last expected spring frost. Check the map to see when that occurs in your area.

Onions—Buy a sack of onion sets (small bulbs) for a quick harvest. Look for little bulbs, no more than one-half inch across. If you plan to eat the onions as scallions, plant the sets two inches deep and two inches apart. Or plan to harvest every other one as a scallion and leave the rest (four inches apart) to grow to full-size onions. They'll be ready for harvest in midsummer.

Peas—Peas grow best in cool weather, but don't plant them in cold, wet soil with poor drainage. They may rot before they sprout. Traditional garden peas (the kind that needs to be shelled) won't produce much food in a small area. If you plant snow peas or snap peas, you can eat the pod and all, but most of these varieties need to be supported. Some edible-pod varieties grow seven or eight feet high and must have a tall fence. Others, such as Sugar Ann, grow only about two feet tall and need no support.

Spinach—As spinach grows, you can cut off the largest outside leaves and add them to salads. The plant will continue to make new leaves.

RECOGNIZING YOUR SEEDLINGS

Weed seeds will be sprouting alongside the vegetables you planted. It's easiest to remove the weeds when they're still small, but you don't want to pull the wrong plants!

Some plants have seed leaves, or *cotyledons* (cot-ih-LEE-duns), when they emerge from the ground. Cotyledons nourish the plant until it begins to make its first *true leaves*. Here's what your young vegetable seedlings will look like:

onion

pea plant

seed leaf

seed leaf

spinach (seen from above)

AVERAGE TIME OF LAST SPRING FROST

The map shows the *average* time of the last spring frost across the United States and lower Canada. The average date for your own garden plot may be different from the one shown for your area. Altitude, the nearness of large bodies of water, the slope of the land, and other conditions affect local temperatures. You can get more exact information from your local Extension Service office (see "Resources," page 46).

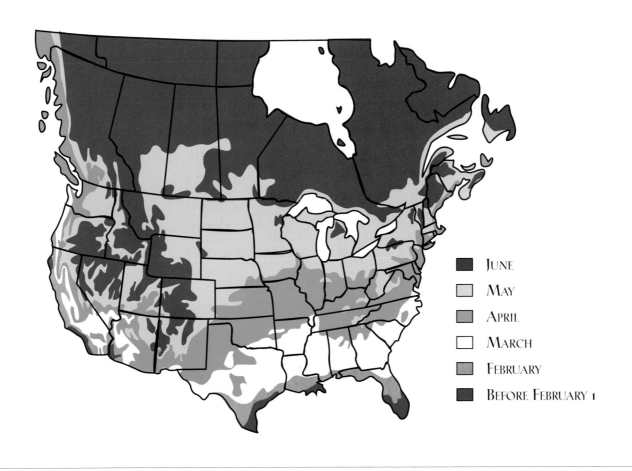

JUNE
MAY
APRIL
MARCH
FEBRUARY
BEFORE FEBRUARY 1

Thinning the seedlings

PAUL'S GARDEN

Plant peas and spinach.

Paul put two tall poles at the ends of his pea furrow and tied rows of twine between them.

LORI'S GARDEN

Plant onions, peas, and spinach.

Lori planted a dwarf variety of snap peas by broadcasting the seeds (scattering them on the bed) about four inches apart. She poked each seed into the ground with her finger. Then she pushed some soil into each hole and patted it down.

APRIL

Onions, peas, and spinach stay free of pests and diseases in most gardens, but keep an eye out for slugs on your pea and spinach plants (see "Pests," page 29).

The cold-hardy vegetables listed for this month can be planted in the garden two to four weeks before the last expected frost. You can also plant any of the vegetables listed last month.

The vegetables that are starred (*) are young plants that are transplanted—that is, moved to the garden after they are partly grown. Because they were started indoors from seeds, they need time to get used to outdoor conditions before they are transplanted. This process is called hardening off. So buy these plants a week or two before you plan to put them out into the garden.

For the first few days, put the plants outside for a few hours in a shady place protected from wind. Increase the time outdoors each day and start giving them some time in the sun. Make sure that the soil in their containers never dries out. In the last days before transplanting, leave the plants outside all day and night. Try to transplant on a cool, sunless day or in the late afternoon.

The plants you buy from garden centers usually have identifying labels that tell how much space you should leave around the plant. Remove each plant from the container carefully, trying not to tear the mass of roots as you pull it out. If you get plants growing in cell packs, you won't have to disturb the roots by pulling the seedlings apart when you transplant them. If the container is made of soft plastic, you may be able to squeeze the bottom like a toothpaste tube and push the plant out. Dig a hole that holds the plant just as deep in the earth as it was in the container. Pat down the soil around the plant, then water it.

Beets—Put some extra effort into preparing the ground where you plant beets and other underground vegetables. For smooth, well-shaped roots, the soil should be loose and well drained. Beets produce a lot of food in a little space, because you can eat the whole plant. The tops make delicious cooked greens.

Cabbages*—These plants need a lot of garden space (about one and a half feet square) and attract a lot of insect pests. You can avoid some insect troubles by preventive action (see "Pests," page 28). Cabbages have a long growing season, so buy plants from a garden shop and put them in the garden after they are hardened off. If you try to grow these plants but get discouraged by heavy insect damage, pull them out and plant something else in their place.

Carrots and **radishes**—These two crops go well together. Carrot seeds are tiny and slow to sprout; radish seeds are large and grow quickly. Try planting both in the same row, one radish seed every inch or so in the carrot furrow. The growing radishes will keep the soil loose for the carrot seeds, and you will be able to harvest the radishes before the carrots need the space.

Leaf lettuce—Some popular varieties that grow quickly are Black-Seeded Simpson, Salad Bowl, and Oak Leaf.

Parsley*—This is another slowpoke plant. Seeds may not sprout for a month, so you may want to buy plants instead. If you decide to start with seeds, cover them with a board to keep the soil moist until they germinate. Keep checking for sprouting seeds under the board and remove it as soon as you see green seedlings.

Turnips—As with beets, both the turnip tops and the roots go to the dinner table.

PESTS

Unless illustrations are life-size, the actual length is shown by ⌐———⌐ .

Cabbage plants and all their plant relatives (broccoli, brussels sprouts, cauliflower, kale, kohlrabi, and collards) attract many insect pests. These four are common and widespread:

CUTWORMS are plump caterpillars that live underground and come out to feed at night. They eat through young plant stems at ground level. Cutworms attack peppers, tomatoes, and other seedlings, as well as cabbages. You can protect young plants by surrounding them with collars at the time you plant them. A collar can be made from a ring of cardboard, a paper cup with the bottom cut off, or a tin can that has both ends removed. Push the collar down into the ground. It should extend at least an inch below and an inch above the soil.

cutworm collar

CABBAGE BUTTERFLIES hover around cabbages and broccoli, looking for places to lay eggs. The small caterpillars hatch in a few days and begin chewing on plants. They match the color of the plants and are hard to see. You can pick them off and kill them, but you have to keep looking for more. Be sure to check the undersides of the leaves.

full-grown
caterpillar

CABBAGE LOOPERS are green caterpillars that move by arching their bodies into a loop. They chew ragged holes in the leaves. Pick them off the plants and kill them.

CABBAGE ROOT MAGGOTS hatch from fly eggs laid in the soil. The small white maggots burrow into nearby plant roots and feed there. Infected plants grow poorly and may wilt and die. You can prevent egg laying by covering the ground around young plants with a mat of cardboard, tar paper, or some other sturdy material. The mat should have a three-inch diameter. Cut a slit in the mat and make a hole in the center that's big enough for the stem. Place the mat flat on the soil around the stem.

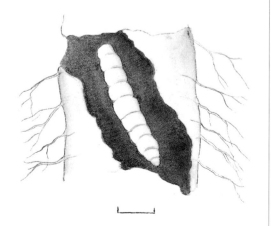

root maggot mat

maggot in root

PESTS (continued)

SLUGS are like snails without the shells. Their bodies are soft and slippery, and they leave a trail of slime as they move. Slugs come out to eat after dark. If they live in your yard, they're likely to invade your lettuce. You can find them on your plants at dusk and pick them off. Use rubber gloves if you don't want to touch them. Or you can lay a board, a shingle, pieces of raw potato, or a cabbage leaf near your plants. The slugs will crawl underneath these objects for shelter in the daytime. Collect the slugs in the morning. You can put them in a plastic bag and crush it to destroy them.

Actual size: ¼ inch to 8 inches

WEEDS

Learn to recognize weeds while they are still small. Here are a few common garden weeds with their seedlings:

common plantain

carpet weed

common chickweed

purslane

yellow wood sorrel

ground ivy or creeping Charlie

BOTH GARDENS
Weed the garden beds.

PAUL'S GARDEN
Plant lettuce in rows that are four inches apart.
Plant a row of radishes.

When the plants are large enough to handle, thin the spinach and lettuce to stand four inches apart, and thin radishes so they are two inches apart. If the spinach and lettuce thinnings are large enough, you can add them to a salad.

Train the pea plants to grow upward by winding the plant tips around the rows of twine.

LORI'S GARDEN
Plant beets, cabbages*, leaf lettuce, parsley*, and carrots and radishes (together).

Thin lettuce and spinach as in Paul's garden. When beets are large enough to handle, thin to four inches apart.

MAY

The date of your last expected spring frost marks the beginning of the warm season. When that day comes, you can plant the crops listed below.

Starred (*) vegetables are put into the garden as transplants.

Basil*—Buy some young plants. Although basil is easy to grow from seed, it's not worth buying a seed packet for just a few plants. Basil leaves —cooked or fresh—are the perfect seasoning for your summer tomatoes.

Green or **snap beans**—Bush-bean varieties are low-growing plants that need no support. Pole beans are vines and need poles, a tall trellis, or a wire fence for support. They require a longer time to mature than bush types but produce over a longer period. If you have no free space for beans now, you can plant them later, after your early vegetables have been harvested.

Pumpkins and **summer squashes**— These gourds are often planted in little groups called hills, but a single plant may be all you have room for in a small garden. Pumpkins are vines. Even the space-saving varieties will spread six feet or more. Summer squashes are bushier, but they may also push out of bounds. If your parents agree, you can plant a few seeds of pumpkin or summer squash in a corner of your garden and let them sprawl onto the lawn as

they grow. Keep only the best plant. Don't worry—even one healthy plant will give you a good harvest. After you thin your seedlings, spread one-foot squares of aluminum foil on the ground around your plant, using stones to hold down the foil. The shiny foil discourages squash-vine borers.

Just to be on the safe side, plant these other heat-loving vegetables a week or so after the last expected frost:

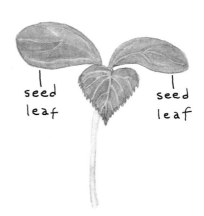

seed leaf   seed leaf

Cucumbers—Even a few healthy plants will produce a lot of cucumbers. If you grow them without supports, choose one of the space-saving bushy cucumbers. Most varieties grow as vines and will need supports in small gardens (see page 32 for information on plant supports). Cucumbers suffer from many diseases, so look for varieties that have built-in resistance.

Eggplants*—These are beautiful plants, with purple flowers, velvety leaves, and shiny dark fruits. Use cutworm collars (see "Pests," page 28).

Peppers*—The fruits of these plants may be sweet flavored or hot, and they come in a variety of colors and shapes. California Wonder, the familiar sweet bell pepper, is the most common variety at garden stores. Use cutworm collars.

Tomatoes*—You can choose a variety that produces large tomatoes or one that grows bite-sized cherry tomatoes. Small tomatoes usually ripen earlier. When planting, remove one or two of the lowest branches on your transplant and set the plant deep in the ground, so the bottom leaves are just above the level of the soil. Use cutworm collars and give the plant some support.

marigolds

FLOWERS FOR THE VEGETABLE GARDEN

Flowers will add color and interest to your garden. Buy a few plants and tuck them into the corners where your growing vegetables won't shade them. These flowers are easy to grow and will blossom for most of the summer:

Impatiens (These don't mind some shade.)
Marigold
Nasturtium (You can put a few of their leaves and flowers in a salad and eat them!)
Petunia
Zinnia

Supporting tomatoes and climbing plants so they can grow upward saves garden space. Vegetables growing on supports will also stay cleaner, and they are less likely to be attacked by soil insects.

Supports should be put in when plants are small. If you have enough room for it, a circle of wire fencing, eighteen inches in diameter and four feet high, makes a good cage for tomato plants. The openings in the fencing must be wide enough so you can put your hands through to pick the ripened fruits. Ready-made tomato cages from garden stores are usually too small to support the tall plants.

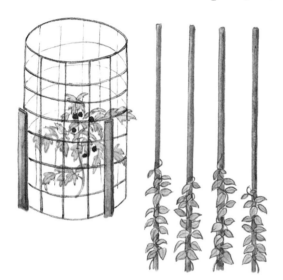

You can also use a pole, such as an old broomstick, pounded firmly into the ground next to the tomato plant. As the tomato grows, keep tying its stem loosely to the pole with strips of rag.

Pole beans and cucumbers climb easily if you give them a little help. Just wind the tips of the young plants around the bottom of the pole or fence to start them. The supports should be at least six feet tall. You can buy tall poles at a lumberyard, but the plants will climb more easily if the surface of the wood is rough. If you use two or more poles in a row, you can run thick twine back and forth between the poles and let the plants climb up the twine.

PESTS

APHIDS are tiny soft-bodied insects that suck out plant juices. They may be green, yellow, black, brown, or red. They usually appear in clusters, feeding on leaves and stems. You can wash them from your plants by using a spray-nozzle hose with enough force to knock the aphids off. Hold your plants in one hand as you spray them, so you don't break the stems. You may have to repeat this treatment a few times.

FLEA BEETLES are small, dark, shiny beetles that hop like fleas when disturbed. They leave tiny holes in the leaves where they feed. Most plants can survive flea beetles without great harm, but heavy attacks sometimes kill young seedlings. If your plants are threatened, try a dose of garlic spray (see "Homemade Spray," page 33).

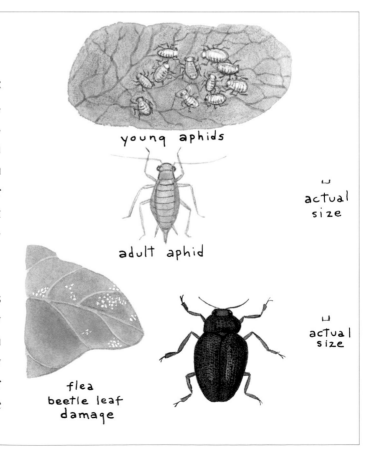

young aphids

actual size

adult aphid

flea beetle leaf damage

actual size

32

HOMEMADE SPRAY

If insects are ruining some plants, try spraying them with this mixture. It's more of a bug chaser than a bug killer. It won't leave a layer of poison on your vegetables the way commercial pesticides do.

Ask an adult to help you chop up some peeled garlic bulbs and a small onion, and then add the pieces to a quart of water. Add a tablespoon of cayenne pepper. Let this mixture sit for a few hours. Strain it through a cloth, and then add a tablespoon of cooking oil or a few drops of dishwashing liquid. Put it in a spray bottle and squirt it on small insect pests. Store the extra spray in the refrigerator.

BOTH GARDENS
Weed the beds.

PAUL'S GARDEN

Harvest spinach when the leaves are big enough to eat. Spinach bolts in warm weather: The leaves stop growing and the plant sends up a thick flower stalk. So try to harvest the entire plant before it bolts.

Radishes usually pop out of the ground when they're ready to harvest.

Because Paul forgot to thin his lettuce, the leaves on the crowded plants never grew very large. He still had some tasty salads from his small lettuce, though.

Plant basil*, bush beans, marigolds*, tomatoes*, and peppers* when the early crops are out of the ground.

LORI'S GARDEN

Harvest spinach and radishes as in Paul's garden.

Lori pulled out some of her onions to eat as scallions and planted basil* in their place. She left the rest of the onions to grow to full size. While harvesting the radishes, she thinned her carrots, leaving one about every two inches.

As soon as the lettuce and spinach were out of the ground, Lori used the space to plant her cucumbers, eggplants*, tomatoes*, zinnias*, and zucchini.

JUNE

Plants sometimes get sick, just as people do. Some insects carry disease to plants as they feed on them. You can spread disease too, by working among the plants (especially beans and peas) when they are wet.

Look over your plants every time you go into the garden. Check the stems and the undersides of the leaves for insects and pick off or wash away the troublemakers before they do heavy damage. Insects may also be hiding out in dead plants, so remove all the old plant parts after harvesting early crops.

If you see a sick or wilted plant, try to figure out the reason for its condition. Is the soil dry? Has insect damage weakened it? Ask the opinion of an experienced gardener, if you know one. If the plant does not revive in a day or two, pull it out—roots and all—so it doesn't infect other plants. Never add diseased plants to your compost heap.

MORE PLANT PESTS

CUCUMBER BEETLES are one-fourth of an inch long and either striped or spotted. They feed on the leaves of cucumbers, pumpkins, squashes, and melons and can spread plant diseases. Pick them off whenever you can catch them and kill them.

The adult MEXICAN BEAN BEETLE is orange or yellowish and about one-fourth of an inch long, with sixteen black spots on its back (eight on each side). It looks like a ladybug, except that the bean beetle has no spots on the segment between the head and body (see page 37 to compare). Young bean beetles are yellow and spiny. Look for adults and young on the undersides of bean leaves. Handpick and destroy them—but be sure you aren't killing a ladybug!

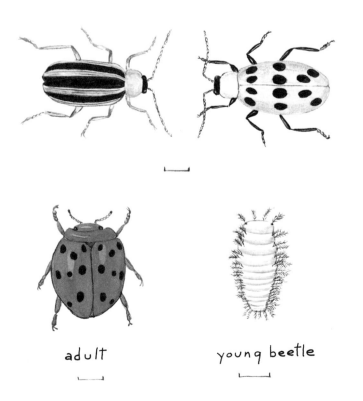

adult   young beetle

Of course, not every insect is an enemy of the garden. Some of them live by feeding on plant pests (see "The Helpful Insects," page 37).

Now that warm weather is here, watering is more urgent. Plan to water your plants whenever less than an inch of rain falls in a week. You can leave an empty can or bucket in the yard and check it after a rainstorm to see how much water has fallen. Try to water early in the morning, before the temperature rises; that way less water will be lost into the air. And give your garden a good soak, not just a light sprinkling.

After the ground has warmed up, you can conserve moisture by covering the beds with a layer of mulch. Use hay or straw, dry (not green) grass clippings, whole or shredded leaves, compost, or some other material that lets water in and holds it in the soil. Mulch also keeps some weed seeds from sprouting.

When tomatoes, squashes, and other summer plants flower and begin to make their fruits, give them some extra nourishment for growth. Compost or manure "tea" is a good fertilizer. To make it, put a shovelful of compost or manure (dry or fresh) in a big plastic bucket. Fill the bucket with water and let it sit for a week. Then dip off some "tea" with a can and water around your plants. You can use the same compost or manure for several batches of fertilizer.

Caterpillars of SQUASH-VINE BORERS enter the stems of cucumbers, squashes, and pumpkins. If a leaf suddenly wilts, look for one of these fat white caterpillars inside the leaf stem near its base. They are over an inch long when fully grown. Cut the stem open, remove the caterpillar, and pile some soil over the injured stem. The plant may recover.

TOMATO HORNWORMS are the giants among garden pests. They are fat green caterpillars that may grow up to five inches long. They feed on tomatoes, peppers, and eggplants. They are hard to spot because they blend so well with the green plants, but you will see their black droppings and the leafless stems where they have fed. Once you find them, hornworms are easy to catch and kill.

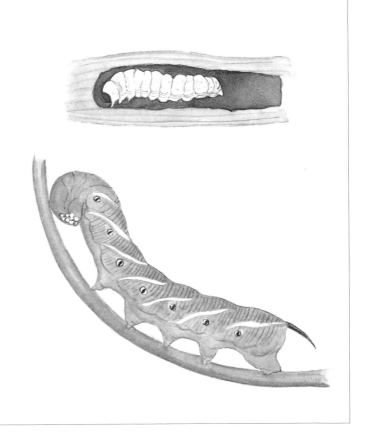

And when the flowers on your cucumber, pumpkin, and summer squash plants burst open, take a good look at the blossoms. All of these plants belong to the same plant family, the gourds. Unlike a tomato or pea plant, many gourd family members have single-sex flowers. Some of their flowers are male (with *stamens*) and others are female (with *pistils*). If you grow any of these plants in your garden, you will see that the first flowers to appear are males. When female flowers appear, you can recognize them by the swollen ovary at the base of the flower.

MALE AND FEMALE FLOWERS

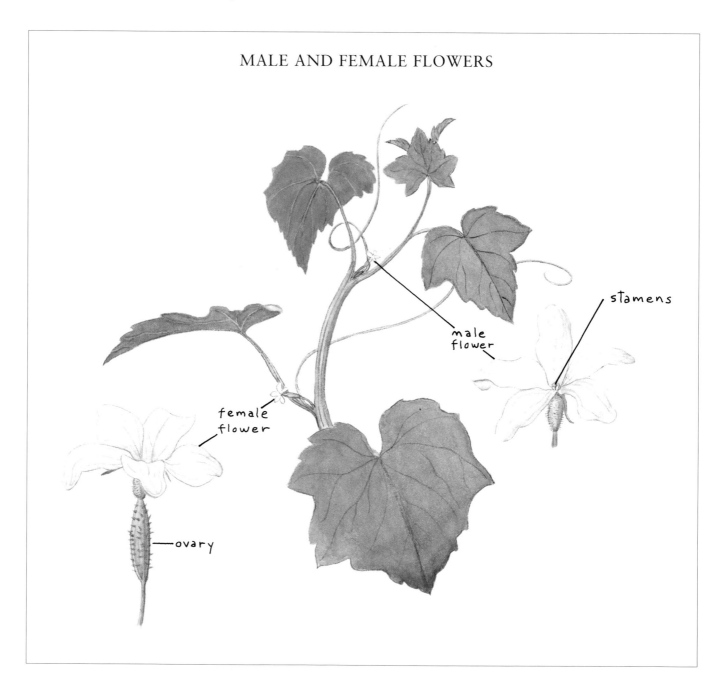

Freshly picked peas—sweet and crisp—are one of the gardener's finest rewards. Harvest them as soon as they are large enough to eat. Always use two hands when you pick peas (and beans), so you don't injure the plant. Hold the stem in one hand while you pull off the pods with the other.

THE HELPFUL INSECTS

All the vegetables that grow from flowers—peas, beans, tomatoes, and others—depend on insects that pollinate them. Without bees and other pollinators, we would have to do the job ourselves by filling a paintbrush with grains of pollen and dabbing every flower in the garden with it! And just as there are armies of insect pests, there are other insects on daily patrol, searching for the pests for their next meal. Here are a few:

LACEWING adults are brown or pale green, with slender bodies one-half to three-fourths of an inch long and delicate wings. Young lacewings are brown or grayish and have a pair of pincers on their heads. The young feed on insect eggs, aphids, and other small insects.

LADYBUGS are the familiar orange or red beetles. Both adult and young ladybugs eat aphids and other small pests. Depending on the species, the young are gray, or black with orange or yellow markings.

Many different species of PARASITIC WASPS lay their eggs on the eggs or caterpillars of other insects. After hatching, the young wasps begin feeding on their host and finally kill it.

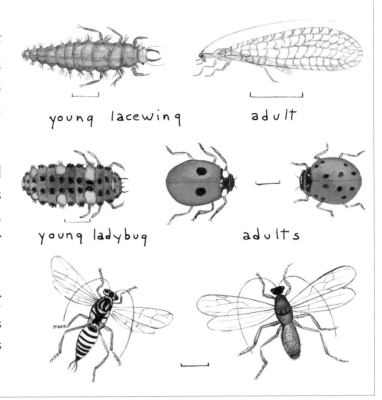

young lacewing   adult

young ladybug   adults

BOTH GARDENS

Fertilize fruiting plants (cucumbers, eggplants, peppers, tomatoes, zucchini).

Mulch the beds, and water and weed as needed.

PAUL'S GARDEN

Paul began picking delicious sugar peas. He used a step stool to reach the pods.

LORI'S GARDEN

Lori started to harvest snow peas. She began to pull some of her carrots as tender "fingerlings"—sweet young carrots as long and thick as a finger—and left the others standing at least three inches apart. She looked forward to harvesting all the carrots soon. Lori was getting tired of weeding between the carrot rows.

JULY

Carrots and beets planted in the spring should be ready to eat. As soon as a garden space is emptied, put in seeds for another harvest. In midsummer, you can still plant beets, bush beans, carrots, warm-weather lettuce (seed catalogs will tell which varieties are heat tolerant), or turnips.

When onion bulbs stop growing, their green tops bend over and become limp and yellow. That's the time to pull out the onions. After harvesting, spread them out to dry in a shady place that is protected from rain. After a week, cut off their shriveled tops and store them.

Your plants will tell you when they are dry. Don't be alarmed if they look a little droopy on a hot afternoon. But if they haven't perked up by morning, give them a good watering.

A layer of mulch saves water as well as work, but mulch is attractive to slugs. Stay alert for slug damage and try trapping them if they are a problem (see "Pests," page 29).

If you are lucky enough to have toads around your yard, encourage them to patrol your garden: Set an old flowerpot upside down in a shady spot nearby, and prop up one edge with a stone. Perhaps a toad will crawl in and use it for a summer home. Toads eat insects and other small animals and are sure to prey on some of your garden pests.

STILL MORE PESTS

The CARROT RUST FLY lays its eggs on underground carrots. As they hatch, the small white maggots tunnel into the root surface. You can still eat the carrot after cutting away the damaged parts.

JAPANESE BEETLES have spread through the eastern half of North America. They spend winter underground as dingy white grubs and emerge as adults in summer. The adults chew on the flowers, leaves, and fruits of a wide variety of plants. Catch and kill them.

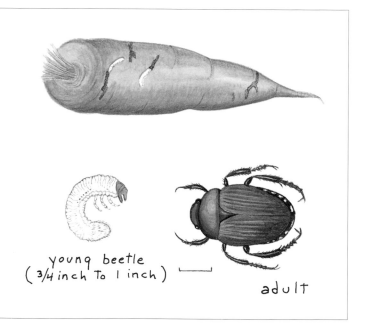

young beetle
(3/4 inch To 1 inch)

adult

But watch out if you touch one! When a toad feels threatened, its skin gives off an irritating fluid. If you get this liquid on your hands, keep your fingers away from your face and wash your hands immediately.

Two common plant diseases may appear late in the season, after plants are fully grown and producing vegetables:

POWDERY MILDEW appears as a gray-white powder on leaf surfaces. The leaves turn yellow and dry up. It can affect beans, peas, lettuce, and members of the gourd family, as well as some floral plants. You can try to halt its spread by removing infected leaves from the garden. Or you can try to avoid the problem by planting resistant varieties, which are available for many (though not all) of the plants affected.

WILT DISEASE causes leaves to turn limp and then die. Once infected, the whole plant should be pulled out and destroyed. You can choose pea seeds and tomato plants that are resistant to wilt. The disease may also affect cabbages, cucumbers, eggplants, radishes, and spinach.

BOTH GARDENS
Water and weed as needed.

PAUL'S GARDEN
Paul pulled out the sugar-pea plants when they became brown and dry and planted a new crop of lettuce in their place. The tomato plants protected the tender lettuce seedlings from too much heat by shading them from the hot afternoon sun. Some of the largest basil leaves went into a batch of spaghetti sauce.

The marigolds look great!

LORI'S GARDEN
Lori harvested onions, cabbages, beets, and carrots. Her snow peas were finished, so she pulled up the plants. She filled the empty beds with new plantings of bush beans, turnips, and leaf lettuce.

Some crisp little bush cucumbers and zucchini were ready to eat.

AUGUST

This is the peak harvest month for summer vegetables. Pick them early in the day, before they begin to lose moisture under the hot sun, and put them in the refrigerator until you're ready to eat them.

Tomatoes taste best if they are picked fully ripe, but beans and cucumbers can be harvested when they are young.

Bean and cucumber plants stop producing if overripe fruits are left unpicked, so harvest beans before the pods begin to swell with seeds and pick cucumbers before they turn yellow. Check the plants every two days and harvest them while they are still young and tender.

Summer squashes also taste best when they are small. It's easy to overlook a zucchini growing under the big umbrella leaves and discover it only when it's a foot long. Oversize squashes are candidates for the compost heap.

Eggplants become heavy, and their weight may cause the whole plant to bend to the ground. You can put in a stake a few inches from the plant and tie either the plant or the stem of the fruit to it with a strip of rag. Or you can place a brick or a flowerpot beneath the fruit to support it. Harvest eggplants while their skins are still smooth and sleek. When they are overripe, they lose their glossy shine. Eggplants are attached to the plant by a thick stem that must be cut with a sharp knife or a garden pruner. Ask an adult to help.

Unlike other vegetables, peppers can remain on the plant even after they are fully grown. They will gradually turn yellow, orange, or red, and after the color changes, they become much sweeter.

Don't let down your guard against destructive insects. Keep checking plants for damage and removing any pests you find.

HARVESTING HERBS

Leafy herbs, such as basil and parsley, will give you fresh seasonings all summer long.

Harvest only the largest outer leaves of the parsley plant. New leaves will continue to grow from the center. Parsley is cold tolerant and will supply fresh leaves even after the first few frosts of fall.

Pick the largest basil leaves to use in the kitchen, and new ones will continue to grow from the tips of the stems until cold weather comes. Late in summer, the basil produces flower buds. If you want to keep harvesting as many leaves as possible, pick off the flower stalks before the buds blossom. Or you can let a few of the flower clusters bloom and set seed, and then collect the seeds to grow your own basil plants next year.

SUMMER SQUASHES

yellow crookneck

yellow straightneck

scallop or pattypan

zucchini

BOTH GARDENS
Water as needed and keep on weeding.

PAUL'S GARDEN
Paul is harvesting beans and juicy little cherry tomatoes.

LORI'S GARDEN
Lori thinned the lettuce and turnips and mulched the new young plants. She is picking cucumbers, zucchini, and beautiful tomatoes.

SEPTEMBER

Many vegetables continue to grow well through the early days of fall, but others may show signs of slowing down. If you pull out some old plants, you may be able to grow a *third* crop in that same bed.

Check your calendar and frost-free date to see how many weeks remain before your first expected frost. Some leaf lettuces will be fully grown in seven weeks. You can plant spinach as late as six weeks before the frost date, and radishes need only four weeks. These vegetables grow well when they are planted after the summer heat is over.

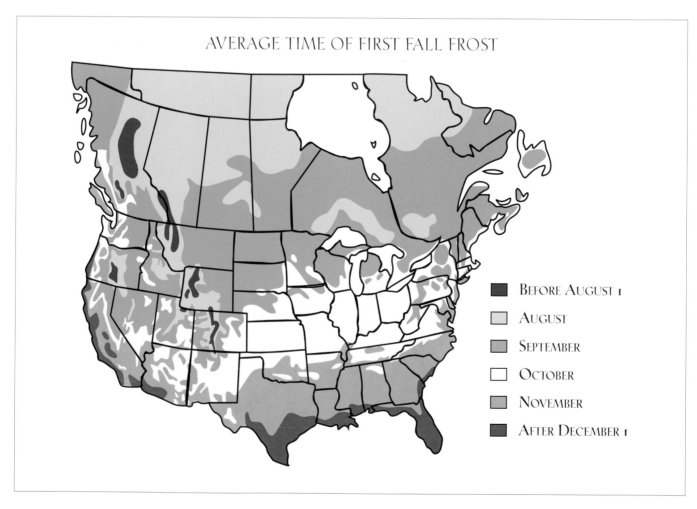

AVERAGE TIME OF FIRST FALL FROST

- BEFORE AUGUST 1
- AUGUST
- SEPTEMBER
- OCTOBER
- NOVEMBER
- AFTER DECEMBER 1

Your garden has been supplying plants with nutrients all summer. If you plant more seeds now, be sure to add some richness to the soil. If you have some rotted compost from your pile, dig that into the soil before planting. You can also use the bagged fertilizer that you bought in the spring, or make a fresh batch of manure or compost tea and pour that onto the bed.

After your last planting, you will probably have seeds left in some of the packets you bought. Many vegetable seeds are good for years (see "Life Expectancy for Seeds") if they are stored correctly. So put the seed packets in a screw-top jar that has a good seal. Wrap a few tablespoons of powdered milk in a tissue, secure the tissue with a rubber band, and put that in the jar with the seeds. (The powder absorbs moisture.) Peas and beans need some air in storage, so put those seeds in a paper bag or, if there is a chance that mice might find them, in a jar with holes punched in its lid. Keep the jars in a cool, dry, dark place until next spring.

LIFE EXPECTANCY FOR SEEDS *(in years)*	
basil 8	parsley 1
bean 3	peas 3
beet 4	pepper 2–4
cabbage 4	pumpkin 4
carrot 3	radish 4
cucumber 5	spinach 3
eggplant 4	squash 4
lettuce 3	tomato 4
onion 1	turnip 1

You may want to experiment by saving some of the seeds you grew in your own garden. Peas and beans, pepper and pumpkin seeds are all easy to save.

But don't try to keep seeds from any garden plant that was grown from hybrid seeds. Hybrid seeds come from plants that have mixed parents—the pollen from one variety of plant fertilizes the ovules of another. If you use seeds produced by the hybrid plant, most of the seedlings will show characteristics of the hybrid's parents rather than of the hybrid plant. Hybrids are usually identified by the word *hybrid* or by *F-1* or *F-2* appearing after the plant's name.

If you save some seeds, try to choose them from the best vegetables on your best plants:

Peas and **beans**—Leave them on the plant for four to six weeks after they ripen, until the pods are dry and brown. Then remove the seeds and dry them in the house before storing.

Peppers—Wait until the pepper turns color and begins to shrivel. Then remove the seeds, let them dry, and store.

Pumpkins—If you didn't grow a pumpkin, save a few large seeds from your Halloween jack-o'-lantern. Wash the seeds and allow them to dry well before storing.

bush cucumbers

BOTH GARDENS
   Harvest ripe vegetables.
   Water and weed as needed.

OCTOBER

If your garden is threatened by a touch of frost one night, take emergency action. Cucumbers, eggplants, tomatoes, peppers, squashes—all the warm-weather vegetables—are most in need of protection. They may survive a light frost if you put them under covers for the night. Drape the garden beds with newspapers, old bed sheets or blankets, plastic sheets, or garbage bags and use rocks or boards to keep the covers in place.

But if the forecast calls for heavy frost, harvest any cold-sensitive produce before the cold snap. Even if the thermometer stays just *above* freezing, long periods at near-freezing temperatures will kill most warm-weather vegetable plants.

You can bring in any tomatoes that are large enough to save. If they have a touch of pink, store them in a dark place, and they will turn red. Of course, they will not taste as good as vine-ripened tomatoes! Take in pumpkins too, before they are nipped by frost. They will keep for a few months in a cool place if they are harvested with an inch or two of stem still attached. Get help from an adult to cut the thick stem.

After the last harvest, pull up the plants and add them to the compost heap. Take out poles, stakes, and vegetable cages and store them inside. And as each garden space is emptied, get your spade and turn over the soil, burying the mulch that covered the bed all summer.

If you still have some energy, here's one crop you can plant before the ground freezes. Buy a couple of garlic bulbs at the grocery and break them into single cloves. Plant them with the pointed end up, two inches deep and four inches apart, and cover the bed with a layer of leaves or other mulch. Their tops may poke up before winter comes, but the cold won't

hurt them. By the middle of next summer, when the tops turn brown, you can harvest a cluster of garlic from each clove that you planted.

Everyone is raking fallen leaves now, so here's your chance to build up your compost pile for next year. Neighbors will probably be glad to let you take their leaves.

Next spring's garden is months away, but now—while all the details are fresh in your mind—make a few notes in your garden notebook to help you plan for the year ahead. What plants did well or poorly? Did you have unusual weather during the growing season (a cold spring, for example, or a dry summer)? Were some plants troubled by pests and disease? How did you solve these problems?

And finally, clean your tools before storing them for the winter. Scrape off the caked-on dirt and wipe the tools clean with a rag. When it's time for planting next spring, they will be ready to go right to work!

CROP ROTATION

Your notebook has a copy of your garden plan to remind you where each plant grew this summer. Use it as a guide when you make next year's garden plan.

After the harvest, pests and diseases may remain in the soil and survive over the winter. If you put tomatoes or carrots in the same spot again next year, any virus or insect that affected those plants will also attack the new crops. But if you shift plants to different parts of the garden each year, the vegetables will have a better chance of avoiding the pests and infections that prey on them.

BOTH GARDENS

Final harvest and cleanup.

And now you and your garden deserve a rest until next spring!

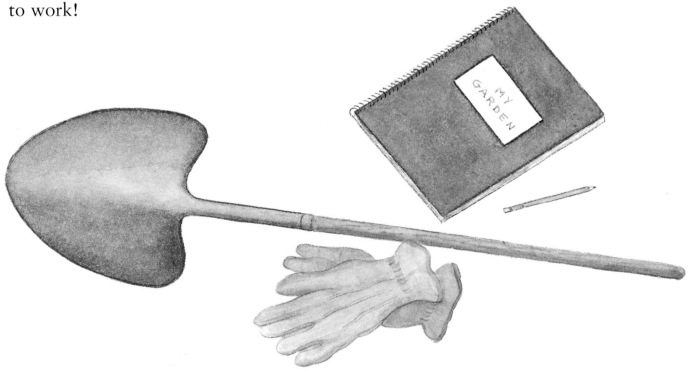

RESOURCES

The Cooperative Extension Service, a branch of the United States Department of Agriculture, has an office serving every county throughout the United States. Your local Extension Service office can give information about frost-free dates for your region, tell you where to send your soil for testing, and help with specific gardening problems. It also distributes publications with advice about planning and planting the home garden.

Help from the Extension Service is just a phone call away, but it may take a little detective work to find the number. Look in the white pages of the phone book under *Cooperative Extension Service* or *Extension Service*. Sometimes the office is listed under the name of the local public university, under *4-H Clubs,* or in the section of the directory that lists governmental agencies.

Canadian gardeners will find Jennifer Bennett's book *The Harrowsmith Northern Gardener* (Camden House Publishing, 1993) a valuable reference. It addresses the special challenges of gardening in cooler climates and includes addresses of Canadian seed suppliers and of soil-testing services in the various provinces.

Look for help in gardening books at your public library too. A growing number of books are devoted to gardening without the use of insect poisons and other chemicals. The titles of these books often include the words *organic gardening* or *natural gardening.* If you discover some mysterious insect infesting your plants, see if you can identify it using your library's resources. You will probably find some books in the gardening section that focus on plant pests. *The Gardener's Bug Book,* by Cynthia Westcott (Doubleday, 1973), is an old favorite. There are more recent books (many published by Rodale Press) that identify insect pests and tell you how to deal with them without the use of poisons.

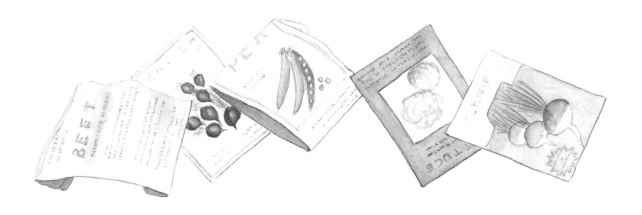

INDEX

Illustrations are in **boldface.**